ANIMALS

COWS

by Emily K. Green

BLASTOFF! READERS

BELLWETHER MEDIA • MINNEAPOLIS, MN

Note to Librarians, Teachers, and Parents:

Blastoff! Readers are carefully developed by literacy experts and combine standards-based content with developmentally appropriate text.

Level 1 provides the most support through repetition of high-frequency words, light text, predictable sentence patterns, and strong visual support.

Level 2 offers early readers a bit more challenge through varied simple sentences, increased text load, and less repetition of high-frequency words.

Level 3 advances early-fluent readers toward fluency through increased text and concept load, less reliance on visuals, longer sentences, and more literary language.

Whichever book is right for your reader, Blastoff! Readers are the perfect books to build confidence and encourage a love of reading that will last a lifetime!

This edition first published in 2007 by Bellwether Media.

No part of this publication may be reproduced in whole or in part without written permission of the publisher. For information regarding permission, write to Bellwether Media Inc., Attention: Permissions Department, Post Office Box 1C, Minnetonka, MN 55345-9998.

Library of Congress Cataloging-in-Publication Data
Green, Emily K., 1966–
  Cows / by Emily K. Green.
    p. cm. — (Blastoff! readers farm animals)
Summary: "A basic introduction to cows and how they live on the farm. Simple text and full color photographs. Developed by literacy experts for students in kindergarten through third grade"–Provided by publisher.
  Includes bibliographical references and index.
  ISBN-13: 978-1-60014-065-5 (hardcover : alk. paper)
  ISBN-10: 1-60014-065-3 (hardcover : alk. paper)
  1. Dairy cattle–Juvenile literature. 2. Cows–Juvenile literature. I. Title.

SF208.G68 2007
636.2'142–dc22
                                              2006035304

Contents

Cows live on a farm.
All cows are female.

Another name for cows is **cattle**. Cattle can also be male. The males are called **bulls**.

Cows have hair
that can be brown,
black, white, or tan.
Many cows have
two colors.

Cows eat fresh grass or **hay**.

May

Cows drink a lot of water every day.

Cows begin to give milk after a **calf** is born. The calf drinks the milk.

Cows give milk through their **udder**.

udder

Farmers must milk their cows every day. Many people drink milk from cows.

19

Cheese, **yogurt**, and ice cream are made from milk. Thanks cows!

Glossary

bull—male cattle

calf—a young cow or bull

cattle—large farm animals; the word *cattle* means both female cows and male bulls.

hay—grass or other plants that are cut, dried, and fed to animals

udder—a bag of skin that hangs under the belly of a cow; the cow's milk flows through the udder.

yogurt—a soft food made out of milk

To Learn More

AT THE LIBRARY

Balan, Bruce. *Cows Going Past*. New York: Dial Books, 2005.

Freeman, Martha. *Mrs. Wow Never Wanted a Cow*. New York: Random House, 2006.

Fox, Mem. *A Particular Cow*. New York: Harcourt, 2006.

Willis, Jeannie, and Tony Ross. *Misery Moo*. New York: Henry Holt, 2005.

ON THE WEB

Learning more about farm animals is as easy as 1, 2, 3.

1. Go to www.factsurfer.com

2. Enter "farm animals" into search box.

3. Click the "Surf" button and you will see a list of related web sites.

With factsurfer.com, finding more information is just a click away.

Index

The photographs in this book are reproduced through the courtesy of: Catalin Stefan, front cover; AVTG, p. 5; Nikita Tiunov, p. 7; Michaela Steininger, p. 9; Lester Lefkowitz/Getty Images, p. 11; Russ Merne/Alamy, p. 13; Lynn Stone/Alamy, p. 15; Steve Humphreys, p. 17; Olga Zaporozhskaya, p. 19; Juriah Mosin, p. 21.